Books in This Series

Better Archery for Boys and Girls
Better Baseball for Boys
Better Basketball for Boys
Better Basketball for Girls
Better Bicycling for Boys and Girls
Better Bowling for Boys
Better Boxing for Boys
Better Camping for Boys
Better Football for Boys
Better Golf for Boys
Better Gymnastics for Boys
Better Gymnastics for Girls
Better Horseback Riding for Boys and Girls
Better Ice Hockey for Boys
Better Ice Skating for Boys and Girls
Better Karate for Boys
Better Kite Flying for Boys and Girls
Better Physical Fitness for Boys
Better Physical Fitness for Girls
Better Roller Skating for Boys and Girls
Better Sailing for Boys and Girls
Better Skateboarding for Boys and Girls
Better Soccer for Boys and Girls
Better Softball for Boys and Girls
Better Surfing for Boys
Better Swimming and Diving for Boys and Girls
Better Table Tennis for Boys and Girls
Better Tennis for Boys and Girls

Better Track and Field Events for Boys
Better Track for Girls
Better Volleyball for Girls
Better Water Skiing for Boys

With indoor competition in the winter, outdoor meets in the spring and summer, and cross-country in the fall, track is a year-round activity.

BETTER TRACK
for Girls

George Sullivan

DODD, MEAD & COMPANY · NEW YORK

PICTURE CREDITS

Adidas, 13 (top); Colgate-Palmolive Company (Duomo), 2 (left), 9, 26 (top), 55; Aime LaMontagne, 11 (right), 53 (right). All other photographs are by George Sullivan.

Copyright © 1981 by George Sullivan
All rights reserved
No part of this book may be reproduced in any form without permission in writing from the publisher
Printed in the United States of America

1 2 3 4 5 6 7 8 9 10

Library of Congress Cataloging in Publication Data

Sullivan, George, 1927–
  Better track for girls.

  SUMMARY: Discusses the equipment, training, and race strategies for sprinting, hurdling, and distance running.
  1. Track-athletics for women—Juvenile literature. [1. Track and field] I. Title.
GV1060.8.S9   796.4′2   80–21399
ISBN 0–396–07911–3

Many people contributed in the preparation of this book. Special thanks are due Ed Sullivan, Girls' Track Coach, West Springfield High School, West Springfield, Massachusetts, and his associates, Sue Herbert and Lisa Nigro. The author is also grateful to these members of the track team, many of whom posed for pictures that appear in the book: Kelly Hutcheons, Tina Groll, Lori Skowera, Robyn Dudley, Carol "Muffy" Eddy, Maria Miller, Ruth Littlefield, Kathy Owen, Kathie Golash, Eileen Green, Debbie Bienia, Eileen Murphy, Laurie McMurdy, Patty Skypeck, Dina Brogan, Judy Connors, Jennifer White, Elaine Baclawski, Phyllis Stevens, Mary Traitiak, Ann Thomas, Alison Burtt, Mary Coulter, Mary Paro, Mary Lynn Green, Nancy Borelli, Peggy Thomas, Sharon Noret, Cathy Paier, Anita LaBranche, Lorraine Burtt, Diane Malone, Julie LaBranche, Heather Handy, Lisa Sapelli, Marcia White, Mary Coughlin, Kelly Gaffney, Darlene Astle, Pam Wall.

The author is also grateful to Connie Meehan, Colgate-Palmolive Co.; Ellen Sweeney, Hoechst Fibers Industries; Sahler Smith, Athletic Director, West Springfield Public Schools; Herb Field, Herb Field Art Studio; Gary Wagner, Wagner-International Photos; Aime LaMontagne, and Bill Sullivan.

CONTENTS

Revolution	8	Hurdle Competition	30
Choosing a Specialty	11	Middle Distance Running	33
Shoes for Running	13	Distance Running	39
Warming Up	15	Relay Races	44
Sprinting	19	Training	49
The Sprint Start	21	Competing	55
Running the Sprints	24	Cross-country	56
Hurdling	28	Glossary	64

REVOLUTION

During the early 1970s, Ellen Cornish, a senior at Frederick (Maryland) High School, ranked as one of the best distance runners among American women. She was a member of the United States team in the world cross-country championships.

Although she was chosen to represent her country in world competition, she was never able to compete for her high school. That was because Frederick High had no girls' track program. And even though she practiced regularly with the boys, she was not permitted to run on the boys' team.

Ellen was once allowed to enter a two-mile race in a dual meet between Frederick and Thomas Jefferson high schools. She was told in advance that she was competing on an exhibition basis, and that any points she happened to win would not count in the scoring.

As the race came down to the final stages, Ellen was battling for the lead. Suddenly a coach darted out onto the track and waved Ellen off. Seeing that Ellen might be going to win, the coach wanted to prevent the boys from suffering the shattering experience of being beaten by a girl.

It isn't likely that anything like that could happen today. For one thing, Frederick High School now has a girls' track program. And boys today don't consider outstanding track performances by girls to be at all unusual. They happen all the time.

New York mini-marathon, with more than 5,000 entries in 1980, ranks as world's biggest sports event for women.

Many factors have helped to trigger the revolutionary changes that have taken place in women's track and other sports. During the 1970s, the women's liberation movement stirred up interest in athletic equality. Women's physical education teachers began to campaign for improved athletic programs for girls. Finally, government legislation, which went into effect in 1976, forced schools to upgrade their women's programs.

The results have been astonishing. On playgrounds and athletic fields and in parks and gymnasiums across the country, girls are running, jumping, hitting, and throwing as they have never done before. Not only are they involved in the traditional women's sports of basketball, softball, and volleyball, but they're also trying baseball, lacrosse, and even rugby.

Track has been deeply affected by the revolution. Consider this evidence:

• In 1972, the first all-women mini-marathon in New York's Central Park drew 78 entries. In 1980, well over 5,000 competitors entered the 6.2 mile (10,000 meter) race, making it the largest women's sports event in the world.

• In 1980, the Colgate Women's Games drew more than 20,000 competitors, ranging from six-year-olds to young adult Olympic hopefuls. Held annually, this event is now ranked as the world's biggest track event.

• On a school level, the National Federation of

Competitors pound toward the finish line in the Colgate Women's Games.

State High School Associations reports that track and field (including cross-country) now ranks as the No. 1 women's sport. In any given year, approximately half a million girls are involved in sprinting, running, and hurdling in interscholastic competition.

With more girls and women competing in track than ever before in history, the record book is taking an awful beating. For example, for five consecutive years beginning in 1973, a new interscholastic mile record for girls was posted. Julie Shea, a senior at Cardinal Gibbons High School in Raleigh, North Carolina, became the latest record holder by running the mile in 4:32.1. But by the time you read this, Julie's record undoubtedly will have been broken.

The same thing is happening on an international basis. In February, 1980, twenty-one-year-old Mary Decker, a former Californian living in Eugene, Oregon, became the first woman to run 880 yards in less than two minutes, when she was timed in 1:59.7 at the San Diego Invitational Track Meet.

That happened to be the third world record that Decker had set that month. She had also lowered the women's record in the mile run and at 1500 meters. Her mile mark was 4:12.7, and she posted a time of 4:00.8 for 1500 meters.

What's ahead for women track performers? No one can say for sure, for the simple reason that no one knows what women are capable of achieving.

Since most women were historically denied the

Julie Shea of Raleigh, North Carolina, holds the mile record for high school girls—4:32.1.

opportunity to train and play sports, only a handful of women have actually reached their potential. As Pat Connolly, women's track coach at the University of California in Los Angeles, said not long ago, "We don't even have any idea how well we can do some things, because we haven't been trying very long."

Successful sprinters are speedsters and have quick reflexes.

Much of what's said above also applies to hurdlers. In addition, hurdlers have to have strong and flexible legs to be able to get over the barriers smoothly and quickly.

A middle distance runner has to have quick reflexes, be a speedster, and have good stamina, too. In junior high and high school, the 440-yard (400-meter) and 880-yard (800-meter) runs are considered middle distance events.

For hurdling, you need strong and flexible legs.

CHOOSING A SPECIALTY

Sprinting. Hurdling. Middle distance running. Distance running. These are the different track specialties. You should pick out one and concentrate on it.

Sprinters compete at distances from 60 yards to 220 yards (200 meters). It takes lightning-quick reflexes to be a good sprinter, because you have to be able to get off to a flying start at the sound of the pistol. Sprinters usually have more natural ability than any other track athletes.

Diligent training will help make you a better distance runner.

Distance running involves competing in events that are 880 yards (800 meters) long or longer. The mile run and the two-mile run are the most popular distance events. In these, the emphasis is on stamina. You have to be able to cope with the fatigue and pain you're going to experience.

In the case of middle distance and distance events, it's possible to make rapid improvement if you're willing to work hard. Indeed, your success may depend simply on the amount of training you want to do, provided, of course, your training program is well suited to your physical makeup and level of ability and experience. The subject of training is examined later in this book.

Once you become involved in track, you may occasionally get confused because some events are described in yards or miles and others in meters. Up until 1981, track competition conducted according to the rules of the National Federation of State High School Associations entailed events described in either yards or miles. But now there is a growing tendency to switch over to the metric system. The 220-yard dash, for example, is being replaced by the 200-meter dash. The 880-yard run is giving way to the 800-meter run. Even the mile, a hallowed distance in the United States, is being supplanted by the 1500-meter run. In time, the problem will be resolved, so that there will be no confusion.

SHOES FOR RUNNING

As running has increased in popularity, so has the number of different running shoes available at local shoe stores. There probably are as many as a hundred different models and styles for you to choose from.

Be careful in making your selection. Buy at a store that specializes in running shoes. Quality shoes cost from $30 to $40, and even more. But it's money well spent. Cheap shoes can lead to painful injuries.

Since most of your running will probably be done on a hard-surfaced track, it's very important that your shoes have sufficient cushioning to absorb the pounding your feet take. The younger you are, the more protection your feet need. Without cushioning, you could be headed for serious foot problems.

To check for cushioning, try on the shoes and run in them, even if it's only a few strides. They should give you a nice springy feeling on each stride. However, they shouldn't be so soft that they feel mushy. Super-soft shoes are just as bad as those with no "give" at all.

At the heel of the shoe, there should be a rigid insert, called a counter. The counter is meant to hold your heel in place, preventing side-to-side movement. The counter should not feel soft or compress easily when you squeeze it. Weak counters invite ankle sprains.

The running shoe you want should bend easily at

Shoes should provide plenty of cushioning.

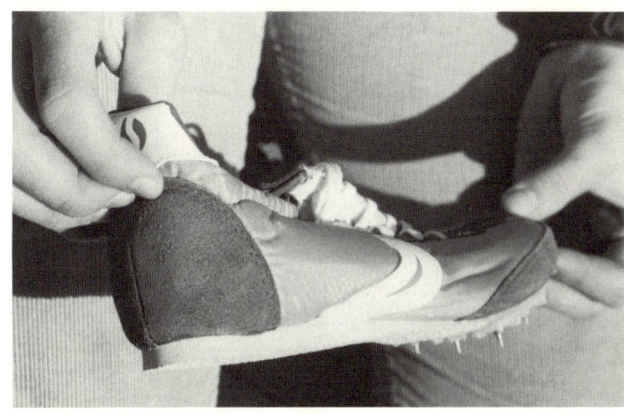

Test the counter; it should be rigid.

the ball of the foot, permitting the toes to move up and down on each stride. Before you try on the shoes, hold the heel of one shoe in one hand, grip the toe in the other hand, and bend the shoe upward. It should flex without any great force being exerted. Avoid stiff shoes; they can cause you to tire quickly, and can result in soreness in the calf area.

When you try on the shoes, be sure there's room for you to wiggle your toes. There should be at least an inch between the end of your longest toe and the front of the shoe. The shoe should also fit snugly at the heel.

If you have unusually narrow feet, don't worry; there are several companies that specialize in narrow running shoes for women. New Balance is the best known of such firms. Besides New Balance shoes, you can try the Adidas TRX or Lady Orion, the Saucony Dove II, or the Brooks Lady Vantage.

If you're a sprinter or a hurdler, you'll wear shoes with sharp nail-like spikes when competing. They're usually arranged in an oval pattern inside the outer edge of the sole.

Test the sole for flexibility.

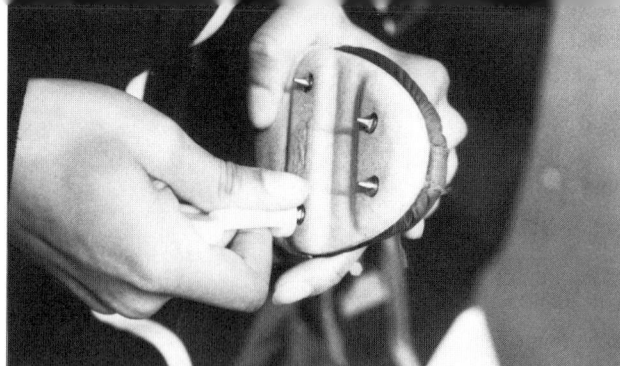

With most shoes, spikes can be replaced.

The length of the spikes is critical, and varies depending on the type of surface on which you run. For outdoor cinder tracks, short spikes are used. These are 5 or 6 mm. in length or about the same length as the tip of a wooden match. Spikes with star-shaped heads are beginning to replace the traditional nail heads.

Quality track shoes have screw-in spikes. You can thus replace the spike that becomes worn or broken. Or you can change the spikes to suit the surface upon which you're racing. A small wrench and a supply of spikes of different lengths are provided when you buy the shoes.

No matter what type of shoes you wear—spikes or those with patterned treads—it's vital that they *feel* good. Don't make your selection on the basis of color or a particular type of side striping. Choose shoes on the basis of comfort. And, remember, if they're not comfortable in the shoe store, they won't be comfortable when you run.

WARMING UP

When young girls begin running, they seem to get more injuries than boys. This is frequently because their muscles aren't as highly developed. Any strenuous exercise can result in muscle soreness.

If you've just joined a track team and started running seriously, don't try to do too much too quickly. Increase the amount of running you do gradually, allowing your muscles to get stronger before you move from one level to the next.

It's also important to prepare your body properly for each running session. Begin your warm-up session by doing about ten minutes of light jogging.

Tight muscles, tendons, and ligaments are subject to pulls, tears, and sprains. Stretching exercises will loosen up your muscles.

Stretching doesn't mean jerking, bobbing, or bouncing. Instead, stretches should be done slowly and carefully, holding your body for a few seconds in the stretched position.

The exercises described and pictured on these pages are especially recommended for runners and hurdlers. Of course, if any exercise causes pain, don't do it, or at least alter it so you can do it without undue strain.

PUSH-UPS—Lie face down and place your hands beside your shoulders, palms down. Raise your body so you're resting only on your palms and toes, and hold it for a count of five. Lower your body and

Push-ups are good for arms, chest, and upper back.

Toe touches can help you develop this kind of flexibility.

Side stretch benefits arm, shoulder, and rib-cage muscles.

repeat. Push-ups benefit the arms, chest, and upper back.

TOE TOUCHES—Begin with your hands on your hips. Thrust your hands over your head as if you are reaching for the sky. Then, bending at the waist, reach down to touch your toes with your fingertips. Keep your legs straight. Return to the starting position and repeat.

Some girls are so supple that this exercise offers

16

Do sit-ups with a partner, interlocking your feet.

In the split stretch, reach first to the right, then to the left.

no great challenge. If you're in this category, touch your toes or even the ground, not with your fingertips but with your palms.

SIDE STRETCH—Put one hand on your hip and arch the other hand over your head. Lean to the right as far as you can, hold the position briefly, and then lean to the left. Repeat several times in both directions.

SIT-UPS—Do this exercise with a partner, interlocking your feet with hers as shown here. Lie on your back, your knees bent. Tuck your chin to your chest and lock your hands behind your head. Raise your upper body until you're sitting upright and then return to the starting position. Then it's your partner's turn. Start with five or ten sit-ups and gradually increase the number.

SPLIT STRETCH—Stand with legs straight and slowly spread your feet apart. Then bend to the right

and touch your left hand to your right toe. Stand erect again and repeat in the other direction.

HURDLER'S STRETCH—Take a sitting position with your legs outstretched. Bend one leg to your side, as you might close a jackknife. Keep the other leg straight. Lean forward from the waist, thrusting your upper body forward, and reaching out to grasp your foot with your hands. Eventually, you should be able to touch your head to your knee. Reverse the position of your legs and repeat the exercise in the other direction. The hurdler's stretch loosens the muscles along the backs of your legs and in your lower back. It's a good drill for every track athlete, not merely hurdlers.

For the hurdler's stretch, begin with one leg at your side, the other outstretched.

The back roll helps loosen virtually all of the body's muscles.

BACK ROLL—Lie on your back and slowly raise your legs with the knees straight, bringing the legs over your head so the toes touch the ground behind you. Keep your legs as straight as you can. Hold the position for a count of five and then ease the legs down. The back roll benefits the entire body, particularly the backs of your legs and your lower back.

When your running session is over, spend at least ten or fifteen minutes doing some light jogging. Cover at least a half mile. Warming down is just as important as warming up.

When you sprint, get plenty of knee action.

SPRINTING

Sprinting is running at full speed. While the best sprinters are blessed with natural ability, there are many sprinting skills that can be learned.

What's important in sprinting is getting your body to work as efficiently as possible as you run. There should be no unnecessary body movement, no wasted energy. Each stride should be smooth and strong.

You must lift your knees high when you sprint.

Take long strides. On each one, drive off the front part of your foot. Pump your arms.

This contributes to the efficiency of your stride.

When you raise your knees high, the lower leg can reach out farther. This longer reach means you get a longer stride. The longer your strides, the fewer you need.

Running with your knees high may not feel natural to you at first. Try this drill: Run in place while holding your hands out in front of you at waist level. As you pump your legs, bring your knees up so they touch your palms. Once you've got the feel of this, try the same drill while jogging.

Once you've developed a high knee lift, begin to

think in terms of increasing the speed of your leg movement. Run on the balls of your feet, driving from the forward part of your foot on each stride. You may have to make a conscious effort to do this at first.

Your arms are important, too. The faster you swing your arms, the faster your legs will move.

Beginning runners often have too short an arm swing. Keep your arms relaxed, swinging your hands to about the height of your shoulders. As your arms swing back, your wrists should go to about your hips.

The arm action should always be straight forward and back. In other words, don't cross your hands in front of your chest. Keeping your elbows close to your sides will help to prevent this.

Cup your hands naturally as you run. Don't make fists. Making fists causes tension in your arms and shoulders. The idea is to keep your body relaxed from head to toe.

All of these skills have to be put together in a smooth and rhythmic running movement. Work on them one at a time and then try blending them together. Once you're able to achieve this blend, your performance can't help but improve.

THE SPRINT START

In short sprints, the race is usually decided by the start. The winner is the girl who gets out of the blocks first. As a beginning sprinter, you'll probably spend as much as half of your training time working on developing your starting technique.

In years past, runners used to dig out shallow holes just behind the starting line to brace their feet when starting. Now they use starting blocks. These consist of adjustable pedals or foot supports that are mounted on either side of a metal shaft.

To get a good start, you must set your blocks correctly. The first thing to do is establish which foot is going to be your back foot. It's whichever foot

Blocks in foreground are set for an elongated start; middle blocks, for a medium start; those at the rear, for a bunched start.

you would use to kick a soccer ball. Or try this: Stand with your feet about 12 inches apart and lean forward. Keep leaning until you're forced to thrust one foot out in front of your body to keep from falling. That foot should be your rear foot in the blocks.

Next, decide how you want the blocks adjusted. You can choose from one of three spacings: elongated, medium, or bunched. With the elongated setting, the blocks are spaced more than a foot apart. For a bunched start, they're only a few inches apart.

Practice starting with all three settings. Choose the one that feels the most comfortable and allows you to dart away easily and naturally.

If you're a beginner, your coach may recommend the medium setting. It enables you to get equal power from each leg.

In short sprints, the starter gives three different commands: "Take your marks!" "Get set!" and "Go!" At the command of "Go!" the gun is fired.

When you hear "Take your marks!" stand with your toes on the starting line, squat down, and put both hands onto the track in front of the line. Then pedal back, one foot at a time, placing your feet firmly against the blocks. Adjust the back foot first, then the front foot. Then draw your hands just behind the starting line. (The rules say that you cannot touch the starting line.)

At this stage, your weight should be concentrated on the back knee, the front foot, and both hands.

"Take your marks!"—Pedal back, placing your feet firmly against the blocks.

"Get set!"—Raise your hips and ease your shoulders forward. Your back should be parallel to the ground.

Your hands should be spread about shoulder-width apart, with the thumb and forefinger of each hand forming a line that is parallel to the starting line. Focus your eyes on a spot two to three feet beyond the starting line. This assures that your head will be correctly positioned. You should be comfortable and relaxed.

On the command of "Get set!" raise your hips and ease your shoulders forward until they're about even with the starting line or just beyond it. Your arms should be straight, but don't lock the elbows.

Your weight is now concentrated on your fingers and your front foot. You should be able to feel the pressure of the starting blocks against the soles of your feet. Keep your eyes focused straight ahead, concentrating on the spot two to three feet beyond the starting line.

You're coiled now, ready to explode away at the sound of the gun. But don't actually listen for the gun. Instead, concentrate on what you're going to do when you hear the gun's sound. This tip will help to quicken your reaction time.

Approximately two or three seconds after the command of "Get set!" you'll hear the sound of the gun. Your body should react instantly, your arms and legs creating a surge of power that gets you into a full running stride as quickly as possible.

Your arms pump hard, one forward, the other back. You push hard from the blocks. But remember to push straight forward, not up.

"Go!"—React instantly, your legs driving, your arms pumping.

Your first strides should be quick and well controlled. They shouldn't be short strides. Make them as long as you can while still maintaining balance and control.

You should cover from 30 to 40 yards before you reach an upright sprinting position and are running at top speed.

Don't try to beat the gun. If you come out of the blocks before the gun is fired, you'll be called for a false start. If this happens once, there's no penalty. But do it twice and you'll be disqualified.

It may help, however, to study the starter. When he or she starts other races, practice starts away from the starting line. This can help you to get used to any special mannerisms the starter may have.

Whenever you practice starts, imagine each to be a race start. Have someone give you the commands, "On your marks!" "Get set!" "Go!" Come out of the blocks as if you're shooting for an Olympic medal. Build up your peak speed before you think about slowing down. What you're attempting to do, besides develop the strength of your legs and your stamina, is make good starts a habit.

To sum up, a successful start depends on a lightning-fast reaction to the starter's gun, coming out of the blocks smoothly and powerfully, and accelerating while well balanced and leaning forward. Stagger, stumble, or fail to move in a straight line and you're almost certain to be behind at the finish.

RUNNING THE SPRINTS

When Chandra Cheesborough was competing at Ribault High School in Jacksonville, Florida, in 1977, she established the girls' national record for the 100-yard dash—10.3 seconds. As this figure suggests, you can't afford to make a mistake in this event. You have to be perfect from start to finish. This also applies to the other sprints. You can't make any errors.

THE 100-YARD (100-METER) DASH—You must have an explosive start in this event, coming out of the blocks as fast as possible (using the techniques described in the previous chapter).

It will take you four or five seconds to reach full speed. Not long after, or somewhere beyond the race's halfway point, you'll begin to tire and start losing speed. This is when you have to put forth extra effort. Pump your arms and drive your legs to maintain as much speed as you possibly can.

As you near the finish line, keep driving. Lift your knees. Drive hard off your toes.

Concentrate on running right through the tape. In fact, imagine the finish to be five yards beyond the tape. Don't throw your hands over your head or

In both the 100-yard and 220-yard dashes, you've got to get out of the blocks fast. That's more important than anything else.

lunge for the tape as you approach it. Simply run naturally.

Some coaches want their runners to lean into the tape. If you plan to try this, lean only from the waist, and only to a degree that feels natural. It's a crime to lose a good race because of a bad finish.

THE 220-YARD (200-METER) DASH—Since this event is run around a curve into a straightaway, a staggered start is used. This means that the runners are assigned lanes, and the starting point for each runner is then adjusted to compensate for the unequal distance each is to run. Suppose you're assigned the inside lane. Then your starting point will be behind the runners in the outside lanes, since they have greater distances to run.

Left: At the finish, run right through the tape.
Below: In the 220-yard dash, a staggered start is used.

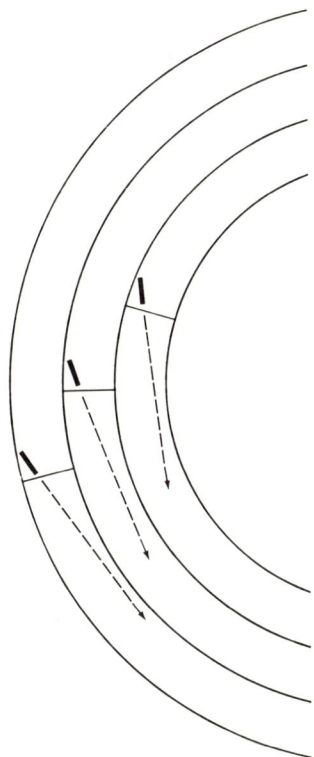

When starting on a turn, as in the 220-yard dash, set your blocks on the outside edge of the turn. Then you're able to run in a straight line while accelerating.

Be sure to set your blocks toward the outside of the lane to which you're assigned. This will enable you to run in a straight line for as long as possible while you're accelerating (see diagram).

This is how to run the 220-yard dash:

Accelerate out of the blocks as fast as you can, just as if you were running a 100-yard dash. Keep running at full speed for 40 or 50 yards.

As you come out of the turn, lengthen your strides. Try to maintain your speed, but with less than full effort.

Over the final stages, drive for the tape. You'll be tired and you won't be traveling as fast as you were at the beginning of the race. But pump your arms. Get your knees up. Work for every last bit of speed.

Not every runner will be able to follow these tactics exactly. Vary them as you like. Maybe you want to delay your final burst to the tape, or perhaps you want to launch it sooner. You can do either.

Don't let the turn in the 220 cause you any difficulty. While you won't be able to run as fast on the turn as you do on the straightaway, you can minimize the loss of speed if you remember two points.

First, run as close as possible to the inside of the lane. Doing so means you run the shortest possible distance.

Second, lean toward the center of the track going around the turn. This counteracts the centrifugal force that you generate when you're negotiating a sharp turn at high speed.

Practice running turns. Begin at a medium speed, gradually increasing your performance. It takes time to get the thigh muscles used to the unusual features of turn running.

Drive toward the hurdle as if you're running a sprint.

HURDLING

The simplest way to define hurdling is to say that it's sprinting over obstacles. It's not a jumping race. The idea is to run fast and glide over each hurdle as it comes.

As a prospective hurdler, the first thing to decide is which leg is going to be your lead leg, the leg that goes over the hurdle first. It's the leg you'd naturally use to kick a soccer ball, or it's the leg you've established as the rear leg in the starting blocks.

Use the same driving start as you do when sprinting. As you approach the hurdle, fix your eyes on the top of the crossbar. Aim your body right for the middle of it. Lean forward slightly.

Driving off your take-off foot, attack the hurdle with your lead leg. Drive the knee up hard and high.

Attack the hurdle with your lead leg. As you clear the crossbar, snap the trailing leg through. Then start sprinting again.

At the same time, the lead arm, the arm on the opposite side of the body, drives forward.

Lean from the waist. Lower your chin. As you clear the hurdle, your lead leg should be fully extended. The sole of the lead foot is aimed straight ahead.

As your body passes over the top of the hurdle, start dropping your lead foot. At the same time, whip the knee of your trailing leg over the barrier. The thigh of the trailing leg should be parallel to the crossbar as the leg clears.

As your lead foot touches the ground, your trailing leg continues to swing forward. Drive off the toes of the lead foot, reaching out into the next stride with what was the trailing foot.

When you're skilled in clearing one hurdle, put a second one 10 yards beyond the first, and start practicing over both hurdles. Take three steps between the hurdles. Be sure the three strides are sprinting strides. If you're unable to reach the second hurdle with three strides, move it closer.

After you've cleared the second hurdle, keep right on sprinting. In so doing, you're practicing your final burst of speed to the finish line.

Once you can clear two hurdles smoothly, try three of them—plus the finish.

HURDLE COMPETITION

Hurdling events for girls are run over several different distances, beginning at 50 yards and ranging up to 400 meters. The hurdles are 30 or 33 inches in height and are officially described as low hurdles.

What are called intermediate hurdles are 36 inches in height. High hurdles are 39 inches high. High and intermediate hurdles are encountered in college competition.

Hurdle races are always run in lanes. You must run in your own lane. You'll be disqualified if you attempt to clear a hurdle in anyone else's lane.

There's no penalty if you should accidentally knock over a hurdle during a race. But if you topple one deliberately or trail your foot alongside the hurdle, that is, not actually clear the crossbar with the foot or leg, you'll be disqualified.

Much of what was said earlier about sprinting applies to junior high and high school hurdle competition. The hurdle events in which you'll be competing are *speed* events. Take, for instance, the 80-meter low hurdles. This event consists of eight hurdles placed 26 feet, 3 inches apart. The first hurdle is 39 feet, 4½ inches from the starting line. The distance from the last hurdle to the finish line is 39 feet, 4½ inches.

No matter what the distance of the event in which you're competing, work out in advance how many strides you're going to take from the starting line to

Think of hurdle events as sprint events. Get out of the blocks fast. Sprint to the first hurdle. Between hurdles, try to take three strides. Each one should be a sprinting stride.

the first hurdle. The idea is to reach the first hurdle on your take-off foot.

If your take-off foot is your left foot, a seven- or nine-step approach requires that you start with the left foot as your back foot in the blocks. An eight-step approach requires that the left foot be the front foot in the blocks. Decide which starting position is right for you.

Remember, at the start, you're a sprinter. Get out of the blocks with bullet speed. Sprint to the first hurdle and drive over it, landing on the ball of your lead foot and snapping the trailing leg through.

Cover the distance between hurdles in three strides, three *sprinting* strides. Run on the balls of your feet. Get plenty of arm and knee action.

If you're unable to cover the distance between hurdles in three strides, try four strides. The difficulty with four strides, however, is that you'll reach the upcoming hurdle on the "wrong" foot, what would normally be your trailing foot. If you can make the switch, that is, use your trailing foot as your take-off foot, there's no problem. If this feels awkward, then shorten your strides and use five of them between hurdles. This assures that you'll reach each hurdle on your take-off foot.

When you clear the last hurdle, sprint to the finish line. Don't ease up until you're well past it.

If you find that you run out of steam before you reach the finish, you'll have to work on building your stamina. One way to do this during practice sessions is to sprint over two hurdles more than are standard for the event in which you usually compete. If you run in an event that requires you to clear 8 hurdles, practice on a 10-hurdle course.

In middle distance running, use more of a flat-footed stride. Always push off from the toes.

MIDDLE DISTANCE RUNNING

In junior high and high school competition, the middle distance events are the quarter-mile and half-mile races. A quarter mile is 440 yards or approximately 400 meters. A half mile is 880 yards or about 800 meters.

If you watched a dozen different middle distance runners, you'd probably see a dozen different running styles. Differences in height and weight make for a wide range of variations, so it's difficult to set down hard and fast recommendations as to middle distance technique.

Some general rules apply, however. Your stride should be shorter than a sprinter's stride. You don't have to have the high knee lift that sprinting requires. Land more on the balls of your feet rather than on the toes, but push off from your toes.

Keep your arms relaxed, the elbows close to the body. There's no need to swing your arms vigorously. Be sure the hands swing straight forward and back and don't cross in front of your chest. Overall, you should strive for an economy of effort.

THE 440-YARD (400-METER) RUN—When competing in a quarter-mile race, you begin from the starting blocks. The race is run once around the track, with the runners assigned lanes and the starting positions staggered to assure that all competitors run the same distance.

The race is run in three distinct parts. Come flying out of the starting blocks, accelerating to top speed as fast as you can. As you come out of the first turn and head into the backstretch, lengthen your strides and try to maintain peak speed, or stay as close as you can to your peak, for as long as you can. When you enter the final turn, you must try to squeeze out a bit more speed for a strong finish.

This may sound difficult. It is. The quarter mile is, in fact, a stern test of your courage. When you enter that final turn and you feel your lungs are about to burst, you must gather yourself for the final drive to the tape. It takes strength and endurance—and heart.

THE 880-YARD (800-METER) RUN—This event, in which you run twice around the track, resembles a distance race more than it does a sprint. You have to have plenty of stamina in order to do well.

Indeed, it takes several months of training to get into condition for the 880 and other distance events, with the program beginning in the fall, perhaps with cross-country competition, and continuing through the winter until the spring and the outdoor season.

The program includes "interval" training and *"fartlek"* work. The chapter in this book titled "Training" explains these terms and makes suggestions as to how you can build your stamina for events of 880 yards and beyond.

In distance races, getting a fast start is not as critical as it is in the sprints. There's no need to crouch down or use blocks. You stand erect at the

"Runners set!"—Position one foot at the starting line, the other behind it. Bend from the waist and at the knees.

"Go!"—Drive off your rear foot. Get your arms pumping. Cut to the inside as soon as it's possible.

start, your knees slightly bent, one foot just in back of the starting line, the other foot to the rear.

The starter gives only two commands, "Runners set!" and "Go!" On "Go!" the pistol fires. Drive off your rear foot, your arms pumping.

Either a staggered start or a scratch start may be used in the 880. If it's a scratch start, with the runners lined up straight across the track, you're permitted to cut to the inside as soon as you want. Of course, you can't interfere with the other runners when you cut to the inside. The rules state that you must be at least two yards ahead of any runner you plan to cut in front of before you make your move.

When a staggered start is used in the 880, you must stay in your assigned lane until you reach the first turn. Then you're permitted to cut to the inside.

After the first turn, you'll be running in single file. Pulling ahead of the runner in front of you takes special tactics.

Forget about passing on the inside. An experienced runner will never let you through on the inside. She can cut you off without breaking any rules. What you have to do is move to the outside and turn on the speed. Once you're ahead of her, steer back to the inside again.

Make every effort to take your opponent by sur-

Do your passing on the straightaways or when coming out of a curve. Move to the outside and turn on the speed.

When you're two or three strides ahead, cut back inside.  Don't ease up; stay in high gear.

prise. Don't wait until you're practically treading on her heels to make your move. Instead, pick up your pace as you approach her. Then swing to the outside, using your momentum to glide right past her. When you're two or three running strides ahead of her, cut back to the inside. But don't ease up. Keep speeding along. You want to bury her, or at least prevent her from answering your challenge.

Do your passing on the straightaways. There's extra distance involved when you try to pass on a turn. But there can be exceptions to this rule. If the race is being run at a slow pace and the runner ahead of you doesn't offer a great challenge, don't hesitate about making your move. And, of course, in the last stages of a race, when you're caught up in a "now or never" situation, you may have to try to pass on a turn.

What should *you* do when someone approaches you from behind?

Run faster. That's basic, of course. You should also move to the outside of your lane. You only have to move a few inches to make your opponent cover more distance.

If possible, try to prevent her from passing, at least until you reach the next turn. She'll have to put forth even *more* effort to get past you on the turn, and may run out of gas.

As a middle distance runner, you have to be able to judge pace—not only your own pace, but the pace at which the race is being run. You have to know exactly how fast you can push your body and for how long.

Some runners make the mistake of finishing fresh. Others run too fast in the early stages, and have nothing left when they reach the final turn.

How do you develop a sense of pace? Trial runs over set distances are one way.

Your coach may instruct you to run four laps, and tell you to run them at an average speed of from 85 to 90 seconds per lap. He or she will stand at the finish line with a stopwatch. As you come by, the coach will tell you your time for the lap, and instruct you to pick up the pace or slow it down.

After a while, you'll develop a feeling for pace. You'll be able to tell within a couple of seconds what your time is over a quarter mile.

For an 880-yard race, you and your coach are likely to decide in advance at what pace you're to run. You may be instructed to run "two 85s," that is, the two laps, each at a speed of 85 seconds.

As the race develops you may have to change your strategy. One or more runners may shoot to the front and start running faster than you expected. The gap between you and the other runners gets wider and wider. You have to speed up; otherwise, you can fall so far behind that you'll never be able to make up the distance. Your strategy has to be flexible when you run the middle distance events.

The critical moment in the 880 occurs in the final lap and usually just beyond the midway point of the backstretch. If you've been running just off the pace, it's at this time that you should begin to launch your final effort.

Don't allow yourself to be boxed in as you move into the straight. You want to have an open road ahead of you. In fact, it's better to be third or fourth in the field, reasonably near the lead, and have a clear run at the pacesetters rather than to be directly behind the leader.

DISTANCE RUNNING

People's attitudes toward distance running for women have changed drastically in recent years. It used to be widely believed that distance running was too much of a strain for the supposedly weaker sex.

That kind of thinking has gone the way of the hoop skirt. In recent years, it's been shown that women can cope with the most rugged of athletic activities. Women now hold many long-distance swimming records for both sexes and have demonstrated they can run men into the ground in ultramarathon competition, that is, in races fifty miles long.

Women are now beginning to achieve their potential in standard distance events. Grete Waitz, an Oslo, Norway, schoolteacher who travels the world to race, is a case in point. In events of 3,000 meters and up, Mrs. Waitz has established records that were undreamed-of just a few years ago. She once ran 10 miles in 51:50.

Her performances as a marathoner have stunned the world of track and field. (A marathon is a race run over a distance of 26 miles, 385 yards.) Mrs. Waitz established the women's world marathon record of 2:27.3 in the New York City Marathon in 1979. That was an improvement of *one hour* over what the best women's marathon time had been only fifteen years before. And with that time, Mrs. Waitz could have beaten half of the male Olympic

When it comes to distance running, Grete Waitz is seldom beaten.

Distance runner's stride resembles a walking stride. The heel touches down first; weight rocks forward to be

winners and *all* the men who ran in the 1970 New York marathon.

Of course, no one is going to expect you to compete in a marathon. In junior high and high school competition, distance races for girls include the mile (1,500 or 1,600 meter) and two-mile (3,000 or 3,200 meter) runs. In college competition, the three-mile (5,000 meter) run is added.

There is no secret toward achieving success at these distances. It is more a matter of conditioning than anything else. If you train harder and more often than your rivals, you should be able to outrun them.

Training not only builds your stamina, but it helps you to become a smoother runner. Even a runner who is ungainly can eventually develop a rhyth-

supported by entire foot. Then push off from the toes into the next stride.

mic and relaxed running style through diligent training.

As a distance runner, you must run with the greatest possible efficiency. Your stride should be relatively short, shorter than that of a middle distance runner or a sprinter. There's not much knee action.

The stride in distance running is much the same as the walking stride. Your heel touches down first. Your weight then rolls forward to be supported by the entire foot. Last, the toes push off into the next stride.

What you shouldn't try to do is run on your toes. That's for sprinters. If you attempt to run on your toes over a long distance, you're likely to suffer muscle cramps in your legs.

Standing start is used in one-mile and two-mile runs.

Some distance runners make the mistake of thumping each foot to the ground. This is hard on the legs and can lead to an assortment of aches and pains. Your heel must come down gently. Then rock forward onto the toes. There should be some spring in each stride.

Be sure to keep your upper body erect as you run. "Run tall" is what one coach tells his runners. Running tall means running with your back straight, your chin up, and your eyes focused straight ahead. This technique helps to give more freedom to your hips, and hip movement is what gives you a rhythmic stride.

Keep your arms relaxed, letting them swing easily forward and back. Cup your fingers.

Breathe naturally, but keep your mouth open. This enables you to draw in as much oxygen as possible with each breath.

DISTANCE COMPETITION—Much of what was said earlier in this book in the section titled "Middle Distance Running" also applies to the one-mile and two-mile runs. Be sure to read the entire section.

In both of these races, you begin from a standing start. When the pistol goes off, drive off your rear foot. Get your arms pumping.

Cut to the inside before you enter the first turn. As you round the turn, you and your rivals will be running in single file. Do your passing coming out of a turn or on a straightaway.

It's vital that you know how to judge pace. In fact, your strategy may be based entirely on maintaining a particular pace. For example, in a mile race your coach may tell you that to win all you have to do is run four 90-second laps.

You may, of course, have to alter your strategy, depending upon what the other runners do. Suppose a rival rushes to the front and begins opening up a big lead. You're maintaining your pace, but she's pulling farther and farther ahead. You'll then have to speed up your pace and attempt to catch her.

Keeping within striking distance is always essential. You can't allow yourself to lose contact with the leader. This isn't likely to happen in a race of 880 yards or shorter. But in the mile or two-mile runs, it's not hard to fall so far behind that you'll never be able to make up the distance.

You also have to keep alert when *you're* the front runner. If your opponents have permitted you to go to the front and stay there, they may simply be allowing you to "do all the work." As the leader, you're breaking the wind. This can be a big advantage for those trailing you.

Keep close check on your pace when you're in the lead. If, after the second or third lap, no one has tried to challenge you, beware. A rival may be running not far behind, getting ready to "steal" the race from you in the final stages. To prevent this from happening, open up as wide a gap as possible between yourself and the rest of the field. As you come out of the final turn and head for the wire, you'll then be able to hold off any last-ditch challenge.

The critical moments in the mile and two-mile runs invariably occur on the backstretch on the final lap. You have to be able to make whatever moves are necessary at this point, so don't let yourself get boxed in as you're rounding the next to last turn. You can prevent this by running just off the right shoulder of the girl in front of you. This strategy also forces the other runners to go even wider when attempting to pass you.

If you feel you have some reserve energy as you enter the backstretch, make your move before the last turn. On the other hand, if you've had to extend yourself to keep up with the leaders, you'll have no choice but to delay your final burst—your kick—for as long as you can.

In helping you maintain your pace, your coach will call out your splits.

RELAY RACES

Relay races are exciting fun. Not only do they require fast running, but also split-second timing by the four girls who make up each of the competing teams.

If you run as a member of a relay team, you'll run one-fourth of the race distance. For example, in the 440-yard relay, which consists of four legs of 110 yards each, you'll run 110 yards.

You'll be stationed at a particular point on the track before the race begins. When the gun sounds, the first runner on your team speeds to where the second runner is waiting and passes the baton to her. The second runner sprints to the third runner, and the third runner to the fourth runner. The fourth runner dashes to the finish line. As many as eight different teams can compete at the same time.

In high school competition, girls usually compete in relay races of 440 yards (four legs of 110 yards each) and 880 yards (four legs of 220 yards). A one-mile relay consists of four legs of 440 yards.

There are also medley relays. In a medley relay, the legs are of unequal lengths. For example, the 880-yard medley relay consists of a 220-yard leg, two 110-yard legs, and a 440-yard leg.

The baton that one team member passes to the next is a hollow cylinder of plastic or metal, about twelve inches in length, and weighing only a couple of ounces. The transfer of the baton from one runner to the next must take place within a designated exchange zone.

Hold the baton like this when you're running.

When a coach is choosing runners to compete in a 440-yard relay, he or she chooses the fastest sprinters on the squad. But it takes more than speed to win a relay contest. Team members have to be very slick in passing the baton. Indeed, in sprint relays, a team whose members can pass the baton quickly and deftly can sometimes defeat a team of faster runners who lack skill in passing.

The exchange zone, 20 yards in length, is outlined on the track by horizontal lines. A second zone, sometimes called the acceleration zone, is 10 yards long and occurs just before the exchange zone. The girl receiving the baton waits within the acceleration zone. As the passer draws near, the receiver begins running. Then, when both runners are within the exchange zone and running at the same speed, the receiver drops her hand behind her and the exchange takes place.

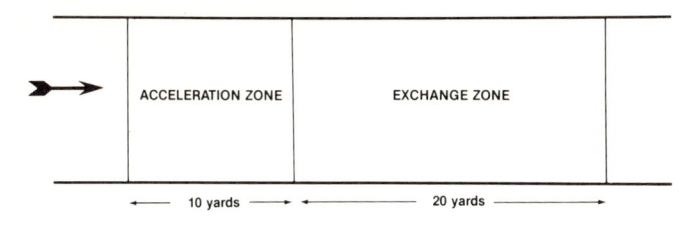

Should the baton be dropped within the exchange zone, either runner is permitted to pick it up. But if it's dropped outside the zone, only the incoming runner is permitted to retrieve it.

The incoming runner must be sure she's holding the baton properly. That's the first consideration in a well-timed pass. She should be gripping the baton by its lower half. The receiver then takes it by the top half. When this technique is used, there's plenty of space for both runners to grip.

SPRINT RELAYS—The 440-yard relay is the classic sprint relay. Each member of each team runs 110 yards.

You use the standard sprint start, breaking from the blocks. The starting positions are staggered.

As you crouch down for the start, hold the baton by one end, grasping it with the last three fingers of your right hand. You'll then be able to use the knuckles of that hand, the thumb, and index finger in supporting your weight.

You can allow the baton to go beyond the starting line. Your hand, of course, can't.

Your teammate, the one who is to receive the

In the sprint relay start, grasp the baton with the last three fingers of your right hand. Use your knuckles, thumb, and index finger for support.

This is a blind pass. Receiver, facing forward, sweeps her hand back at the command of "Now!" to accept baton

baton, will be waiting at a point about midway in the first turn. When you break from the blocks and approach that turn, hitting a checkpoint that you and she have established in advance, shout out, "Go!" On that command, the receiver takes off.

When you're both within the exchange zone and running at the same speed, call out "Now!" or "Hand!" On that command, the receiver, still facing forward, sweeps her hand back. Place the baton across the "V" formed by her thumb and forefinger.

The exact point within the exchange zone where the exchange takes place depends on how quickly the receiver can reach top speed. But the transfer should occur as early as possible in the exchange zone. If a mistake should then occur, you'll have time to correct it.

from incoming runner.

Once the pass has been completed and the receiver is on her way, stay in your lane until you've checked traffic conditions. There may be other runners in adjacent lanes. By crossing lanes when leaving the track, you can cause a collision. If it's your fault, your team can be disqualified.

This is called a "blind" or nonvisual pass because the receiver doesn't actually see the exchange being made. She's facing forward, concentrating on getting away fast.

When you're a receiver, waiting in the acceleration zone as your teammate comes charging toward you, face in the direction you're going to be running. One foot is well ahead of the other; your knees are bent. It's much the same position that runners use in a distance race start.

Don't turn and try to peek over your shoulder at the incoming runner. You must learn to trust the other runner. Turning your head not only slows you down, but it can cause you to twist your hand. That's bad; you must keep your hand flat in order to assure a trouble-free exchange.

Your coach will announce in advance which hand each member of the team is to use in passing and receiving. The most efficient method involves a right-to-left-to-right-to-left exchange. The first runner carries the baton in her right hand and passes to the left hand of the second runner. The second runner passes to the right hand of the third runner. She, in turn, passes to the left hand of the fourth runner.

It may feel awkward for you to receive and carry the baton in your left hand. You're not confident; you may think you're going to drop it during an exchange. In such a case, the coach may change the running sequence of the members of your team so that you're able to receive the baton with your right hand. Or he may assign you to run the first leg, in

In distance relays, a visual exchange is used. Receiver looks back to help assure a trouble-free pass.

which case you won't have to do any receiving at all.

In order to achieve smooth exchanges, you and your teammates must do plenty of practicing. If you play the role of both a receiver and a passer during a race, then you must work on both of those roles in your practice sessions. Strive to make all your movements as natural as possible. For example, when you thrust one hand forward in passing the baton, it should be the hand that is naturally moving forward at that instant. If you're striding forward on the left foot, then it's your right hand that's going forward. In other words, all the hand and arm movements you use in both passing and receiving should simply be extensions of the movements you use when running.

DISTANCE RELAYS—As relay distances get longer, the necessity of fast baton exchanges diminishes. This is because the incoming member of the team, having run a considerable distance, is likely to be at the point of collapse. A smooth, well-coordinated exchange simply isn't possible.

What's called a visual exchange is used in distance relays. If you're the receiver, you're responsible for a trouble-free exchange. Face forward, but turn to look back over your shoulder as your teammate approaches.

When the incoming runner arrives, she's supposed to extend her hand, offering you the baton. But she may be on the brink of exhaustion and unable to do this. It's then up to you to reach out and take the baton from her. Concentrate on not dropping the baton. That's what's vital.

Your coach will decide in advance the order in which the girls on your team will run. In so doing, he or she will try to use each girl's skills to the best advantage. For instance, a girl who can start fast is likely to be the first runner. Girls who are quick and sure-handed in handling the baton may be slotted to run either second or third, since these slots involve both passing and receiving the baton.

Oftentimes, however, running speed is the sole criterion the coach uses in setting the sequence of runners. The second fastest runner will be assigned to run first. The fastest runner will be assigned to run fourth, anchoring the team. It's her job to finish first, whether that involves holding onto a lead built by the other runners or closing any gap that's opened.

TRAINING

Through proper training, you can improve your speed and increase your strength. As a result, you'll perform better.

It's important that you enjoy training. There will be days when you should work hard in preparing for an event. But there will also be days when you shouldn't do any work at all. Training shouldn't be drudgery. If you don't get enjoyment out of what you're doing, you'll never be able to do your best.

It's usual for a young woman to reach her peak as a runner at the age of 24 or 25. That means that you're now becoming involved in a program that may be going to last another ten years or so before you can expect to begin achieving your ultimate goals. What this means is that you shouldn't try to rush your development. Be patient. Take your time developing your skills. Enjoy yourself.

In developing a training program for yourself, consult your coach or trainer. Talk with your friends and other runners. Find out what kind of training they do. Then work out your own program, one that's tailored for your needs and capabilities.

Whether you're a sprinter or a distance runner, the training program you follow will vary from month to month, the idea being to bring you to a fitness peak during the competitive season. In the off-season, you'll be more involved with distance running, that is, with building your stamina. As the competitive season draws near, your conditioning

Interval training involves alternate fast running and jogging over set distances.

program becomes more intense and you'll work more toward perfecting the skills important to your event. During the season, you'll spend most of the time working on your specialty, plus performing whatever drills are necessary to keep you at a fitness peak.

Your program is sure to include an assortment of different training techniques. One of these is interval running, which involves alternately running and jogging over set distances. When using this technique, you can vary the distance you run, the number of times you run it, the speed at which you run, and the amount of time spent jogging between runs. You can thus make interval training as easy or as demanding as you want.

The set distance you'll be assigned to run will probably be less than the distance you run in competition. For example, if your specialty is either the 100-yard or 220-yard dash, your coach may have you run four 60-yard sprints from the blocks during a training session, walking 60 yards between each of the sprints. A middle distance runner might be assigned to run 220-yard or 440-yard intervals. A miler might run intervals of 440 or 880 yards.

As you can judge, interval training not only does much to build stamina, but it also works to condition the body for the strain and fast pace of sprinting.

Fartlek running is another training technique your coach is likely to recommend. *Fartlek* is a

Fartlek training, which can include uphill work, helps build stamina.

Swedish word that means "speed play." It involves covering long distances, from two to five miles, say, over a cross-country course terrain, while alternately sprinting and jogging.

On a typical *fartlek* outing, you might jog for five or ten minutes, run at close to top speed for a quarter of a mile, and then jog easily for several minutes. You can also mix in some rapid walking, an uphill run or two, and a few short sprints.

Exactly what you do and for how long depends upon your capabilities and the event for which you're training. It goes without saying that *fartlek* training builds stamina. Thus, middle distance and distance runners find it especially beneficial.

While *fartlek* and interval training are good for building endurance, weight lifting increases strength. Don't think of weight lifting in terms of trying to pick up 250 pounds from the floor. Lifting can be as simple as a drill called the arm curl which involves exercising with a hand-held barbell that can weigh as little as five pounds.

Distance runners sometimes lift weights to develop the strength of their upper bodies. Sprinters and hurdlers use weights during the off-season to help them keep in shape.

But don't undertake any weight lifting program

Weight training can be helpful, too. But be sure you're supervised.

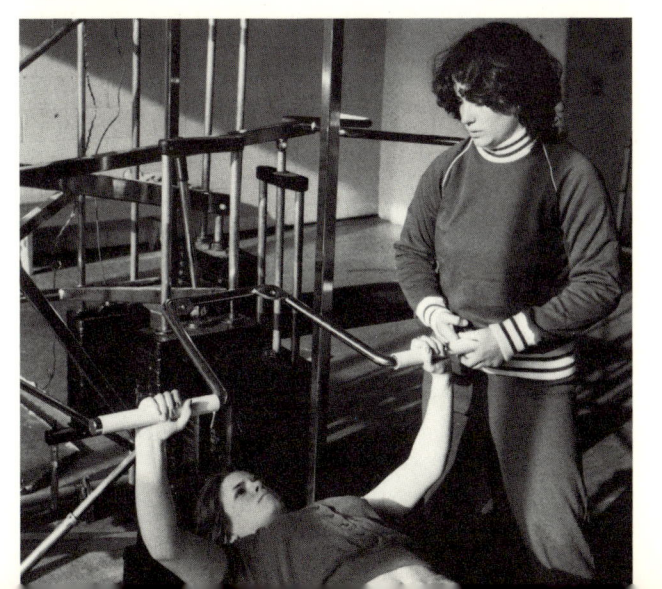

without proper instruction and supervision. By failing to use the proper techniques, you can strain or otherwise seriously injure yourself.

Whatever kind of program you develop for yourself, don't follow it slavishly. This is especially true if you're a beginner. If a practice session is so rigorous that you ache and feel tired the next day, cut the amount of work you're doing. Increase it gradually as you build your strength and stamina.

"Listen to your body." That's the advice that experienced runners give. Your body will tell you when it needs to be rested. It will also tell you when you can go long and hard.

SPRINTING—Starting. Finishing. Stride development. Technique. If you're a sprinter, these are some of the things you'll be concerned about during your training sessions. You'll probably work out five or six days a week, training at least an hour a day.

The best way to train yourself to run fast is to run at top speed, or at close to top speed, as often as you can. Because sprinting is an all-out effort, the muscles involved get stronger only when worked at close to the limit. It's the same as in weight lifting. The lifter must lift the maximum weight possible in order to develop increased muscular strength. It's only by running as fast as you can that you develop your running muscles.

This means that a good amount of your time is going to be spent simply getting your breath back, that is, recovering. Slow jogging is one way to recover. You have to recover fully. There's nothing to be gained by running fast if your body isn't fully rested after the previous sprint.

Every training session should begin with a warm-up jog that lasts about ten minutes. Don't do any fast running yet. You're just trying to loosen your muscles.

Next, spend about ten minutes doing stretching exercises. Several such exercises are described and pictured earlier in this book.

When you're warmed up, don your spikes and run four 100-yard dashes out of the blocks. Be sure to recover fully from one before going on to the next.

Then run four 50-yard dashes, again out of the blocks. This time concentrate more on form, on getting power and speed into the movements of your legs.

Next, practice four starts, running until you reach full speed on each. Practice some finishes, too. On each, run right through the tape.

If you have any particular weakness, you should work on overcoming it. Maybe you have a tendency to slow down on the turns. If so, practice some turn running, putting added emphasis on generating good speed.

Last, jog slowly around the track, giving your body a chance to warm down. Warming down is just as important as warming up.

HURDLING—Sprint training, even sprint com-

Hurdlers unlimber with this stretching exercise.

petition, is essential for hurdlers. In fact, you should think of yourself, not merely as a hurdler, but as a sprinter whose specialty happens to be running over obstacles.

Besides sprint training, there are special exercises you should do that will help you increase the flexibility your body must have in order to be a successful hurdler. One calls for you to simply stand to one side of the hurdle crossbar, face it, and then pass first one leg and then the other over the crossbar.

Another good stretching exercise involves standing in front of the crossbar and placing one foot atop it. As you reach forward to grasp your toes, slowly bend your head toward your knee. Then switch legs and repeat the exercise.

Before you begin actually going over the hurdles, try this drill: Approach a hurdle at close to your normal rate of speed, but plan to pass the hurdle on one side. Plant your take-off foot well to the left of its normal spot, stride with your lead foot, and then snap the trailing leg over the crossbar. In other words, only the trailing leg actually goes over the

Going by the hurdle on one side and snapping the trailing leg over it is a good warm-up drill.

hurdle. This drill gives you confidence in the movement of your trailing leg and prepares the way for practicing over the hurdles in normal fashion.

MIDDLE DISTANCE AND DISTANCE RUNNING—Training programs for middle distance and distance running vary widely. One reason for this is because distance runners themselves cover a wide range in terms of ability. Different runners succeed with different systems. Some stress hard work and interval training. Others put the emphasis on distance running.

Most coaches want their distance runners to do at least some interval training, often repeating 440-yard or 880-yard runs. Maybe as much as fifteen minutes of each of two training sessions every week will be devoted to interval training.

During the competitive season, interval training is done early in the week, at least two or three days before any scheduled meet.

Training for distance runners includes plenty of *fartlek* work. For as long as an hour, you run over hill and dale, sometimes sprinting for distances of 20 to 25 yards, other times jogging easily. You never stop moving for that hour.

Taper off toward the end of the week as race day draws near. The day before the race, you might do a half hour of light jogging. Or you might rest.

The day after competition, it's wise to do up to an hour of light jogging, just to keep your muscles loose.

Whether you're a distance runner or a sprinter, keep in mind that no training session should ever be so demanding that you cannot train properly the next day. Nor should it be such a snap that it has no real effect on your speed, strength, or stamina. It's up to you to find the middle ground.

COMPETING

On the day of the race, when you hear the starter's command, "Take your marks!" you're sure to feel butterflies fluttering in your stomach. Don't worry. Being excited and a little nervous before a race is normal. Every runner experiences some anxiety, even world champions.

As you become skilled and experienced in your event, you should begin feeling less nervous. But it's not likely the feeling will ever leave you entirely.

Start preparing yourself mentally in the days before the race is scheduled. Think in positive terms about what you plan to do. If you're a sprinter, have a mental image of how you're going to come exploding out of the blocks and go driving for the finish line with long, powerful strides. If you're a hurdler, picture yourself soaring elegantly over the barriers. A distance runner should think of herself running with the speed and grace of a nimble-footed doe.

Get a good night's sleep before the race.

On race day, watch what you eat. The final meal before the race should consist of foods noted for their carbohydrates. Carbohydrates can be found in potatoes, fruits, sugar, rice, pasta, and bread. These supply the body with energy.

Avoid protein-rich foods—meat, fish, eggs—in the hours before a race. Such foods are harder to digest.

After the race is over, sit down with your coach

There's nothing like winning—but there can be only one winner.

and talk to him or her about it. What did you do right? What did you do wrong? What should you do to improve? You should learn something from every race.

Don't feel badly if you don't win. There can only be one winner. Knowing that you've done your best should give you personal satisfaction, whether you win or lose.

Team unlimbers before cross-country meet.

CROSS-COUNTRY

Cross-country, a term that is short for "cross-countryside," is distance racing over natural terrain—through parks and over wooded trails. You're far from any track or engineered roads.

In the late 1800s, when baseball was beginning to develop in the United States, cross-country was starting to become popular in England. By 1890, the sport had been transplanted to the United States and championship races were being held here under the sponsorship of the Amateur Athletic Union (the AAU). From American colleges, interest filtered down to the high school level. In New York City, high schools were offering cross-country as early as 1907. Today, of course, bustling cross-country programs for girls and boys are available in high schools everywhere. Traditionally, competition begins not long after school opens in the fall.

Girls' high school teams run distances of from one to five miles, depending on the age and experience of the competitors. Cross-country is always a team sport, usually with seven girls to a team. As a member of a team, your order of finish determines your contribution to the team score. One point is given for finishing in first place, 2 points for second place, 3 points for third, 12 points for twelfth, and 142 points for 142nd place. (There can, indeed, be 142 competitors in a race; many more than that, in fact.) Only the scores of the first five finishers for each team are counted. The team with the lowest score wins.

Since terrain and race conditions vary so greatly from course to course, times mean little in cross-country competition. You'll be confronted with winding paths, sharp turns, and steep hills. You can cover farmland or sections of rural roads. Many high school races are conducted over golf courses. In Hawaii, there's one cross-country course that winds through the grounds of a hospital and a cemetery, and another that leads through the surf and sand of famous beaches. So cross-country tests not only your speed and stamina, but your adaptability as well.

Cross-country races sometimes involve hundreds of competitors. This is a race start at Van Cortlandt Park in New York City.

Van Cortlandt course is typical, winding over and through thickly wooded terrain.

Most of your competition will come during dual meets, wherein your team competes against another school. But your team will also compete in invitational meets. These will often involve hundreds of runners from dozens of schools. In many states, there are district, sectional, and regional meets. The grand championship is usually the state finals. As a member of a school team, you'll probably participate in as many as ten cross-country races each season.

Some cross-country events are of enormous size. Mount San Antonio College in California sponsors an annual cross-country extravaganza for colleges, high schools, grade schools, and novice runners. More than 6,000 athletes take part.

Almost as big is the annual cross-country meet offered by Manhattan College at Van Cortlandt Park in New York City. In one recent year, more than 5,000 girls and boys representing 250 schools from nine northeastern states competed in the event.

RUNNING FORM—When you're running a cross-country course and have a long distance to cover, you may be tempted to use long strides. But long strides will cause you to "bounce" up and down. When the terrain is uneven, you'll waste a good deal of energy simply trying to keep your balance. So keep your strides short, the foot always landing below the body, not out in front of it. This is the efficient way to run.

Also check your arm movement. Your arms should be relaxed and allowed to swing from the

Work for an efficient stride, with good arm action.

shoulders with the elbows bent. And, as in sprint or distance running, the hands should move forward and back. If you allow the hands to cross in front of your chest, it can cause your whole body to rotate from one side to the other. You'll waste valuable energy as a result.

Always keep your upper body erect when you run. If you lean forward, you'll have to use extra energy in trying to maintain your balance. Leaning back can cause you to bounce up and down and robs your stride of its propulsion. You'll be "spinning your wheels."

For hills, which are found along virtually every cross-country route, you must modify your running form. Shorten your stride and lean into the hill slightly, springing from the ankles and toes as you drive your arms powerfully. Try not to look toward the top of the hill as you run, since this can distort your posture.

Don't think in terms of "attacking" the hill. All you should try to do is maintain your pace. This should enable you to "run through" the top of the hill, and then glide down the other side, letting gravity do some of the work. As you speed downhill, try to keep your body perpendicular to the ground.

Here are some additional cross-country tips:

• Good running shoes (described earlier in this book) are a must. They should give you plenty of support at the heel. A ridged or waffle-soled tread should provide sufficient traction. Some runners, however, prefer spikes. They cost more, of course, but they may be something of a necessity if the course is wet and you expect to encounter bad footing.

High socks are sometimes recommended. They can prevent scratches from bushes or branches.

• Be sure to "read" the course before you run it in competition. Where are the hills and other obstacles? What kind of footing does it offer? Are there "blind" stretches that will cut off your view of the

Going downhill, you can let gravity do some of the work.

leaders? Are there sharp turns? Is the route clearly marked? The only way you can get answers to these and similar questions is by running the whole course in advance, maybe a day or two before the competition is scheduled. Even if you arrive at the race site only an hour or two before the start, you should look over as much of it as you can.

• Try to find out as much as possible about the opposition runners. When a rival shoots into the lead, you have to know whether she's capable of "stealing" the race. On the other hand, she may have a history of tiring and folding. This kind of knowledge enables you to plan your own strategy intelligently.

• When you pass a rival runner, do so decisively. As you glide by, try picking up the speed, putting as much daylight as possible between yourself and the opponent. While she will feel defeated, you'll be more encouraged to catch and pass the *next* runner.

• Many cross-country courses consist of a long, hilly, thickly wooded portion that is sandwiched between wide, open areas at the start and finish. When you're running over a course of this type, it's vital to get out in front at the start. If you lag behind, you may find it impossible to make up any yardage on the crowded footpaths you're going to encounter when you reach the hills.

• You can pick up half a stride or more on your opponents by learning how to negotiate sharp turns. Several strides before you reach the turn, thrust

Finding out as much as you can about the leading runners will help you in planning your strategy.

your outside shoulder forward and pull your inside shoulder back. Then, as you reach the turn, lean into it slightly. At the same time, bring your lower body and legs in alignment with your shoulders. This enables you to "slide" around the turn as you run. There's no breaking stride.

• "To run well in cross-country," one coach tells his runners, "you have to remember there is something to do at all times. You should be trying to catch someone, prevent someone from catching you, or be working to maintain your pace in the face of hills, turns, and narrow pathways. Concentrating for the whole race is necessary to be successful."

TRAINING—There are many similarities in train-

Having far outdistanced the field, cross-country winner hits the tape.

61

ing for cross-country and track training. In both, you try to achieve a certain level of fitness, developing both the strength of your legs and your stamina.

The chief difference between the two is *where* you train. Instead of working out on a track, you do your running on natural terrain, getting ready for the hills and rough ground you're going to encounter by making them a part of your daily training schedule.

Most coaches of high school teams divide cross-country training into three stages: First, there's preseason conditioning, which usually lasts from six to eight weeks. Most coaches consider this to be the most important part of the training program. Second, there's early-season development. Third, there's a sharpening phase in which your skills are brought to a competitive peak.

If your most important cross-country events are scheduled for late in the fall, you should begin training in July. Do your stretching exercises daily. Do some strength exercises three or four times a week. Sit-ups and push-ups are good strength exercises. Run as often as you can. If it's possible for you to get out on a cross-country course six times a week, do it. Try to cover at least twice the race distance you'll be running in the fall. If your school's cross-country course is 1½ miles in length, then you should run at least 3 miles a day.

You might want to consider attending a running camp during the summer. There are dozens of these, many of which are described in the various magazines and newspapers devoted to running. While many camps stress track and field, there are others that put the emphasis on distance running and cross-country.

Some camps are based on grounds used by all-purpose camps. Others are situated on school or college campuses. Besides location, facilities, and cost, be sure to consider the number of instructors available and the quality of the instruction staff before making your choice.

If you attend a camp, expect to take part in long workouts every day. You'll also receive topflight instruction. And you'll do everything in the company of other runners like yourself.

One word of caution: If you're merely pretty much a beginner in distance running, and cover 12 to 14 miles a week or thereabouts, don't sign up for a camp where the athletes run two or three times a day and make it a habit of logging 20 miles or so. For a beginner, such a program can do more harm than good.

In the early weeks of the cross-country season, your training program should increase in intensity. If you're running three or four miles a day, your coach may recommend that you step up your distance to six miles, or maybe more. He or she may also advise that you do some interval training (described earlier in this book). For example, you may be advised to run several half-miles at specific times.

This part of your training program is meant to enable you to handle fast race paces.

In the final phase of your program, your coach is likely to advise you to cut down on the amount of distance work you're doing and put a greater stress on interval training. For instance, Mondays and Wednesdays may become "hard" days in which you do shorter intervals for briefer periods. This routine should bring you to a peak in terms of speed and stamina.

In the late fall, you may begin to encounter some cold days. You can run safely in cold weather. Simply dress properly. Wear thermal underwear, leotards, a long-sleeved turtleneck, warm-up pants, a hooded sweatshirt, and thermal socks. But wear just enough to keep yourself warm. Don't weigh yourself down.

Don't fail to protect the most vital parts of your body—your head, wrists, and hands. As much as 30 percent of the body heat escapes through the head. Keep it covered on cold days with a wool hat or hooded sweatshirt.

When it's bitter cold, you may want to wear a ski mask to protect your face from frostbite.

Keep your hands inside a pair of mittens. Be sure they're long enough to cover your wrists.

There may be some days when snow falls. Unless it gets very deep, try to stick to your training routine. If you usually run an hour, continue to run that amount of time, even though you may cover only half the distance.

Ice is another matter. You can slip and injure yourself. When conditions become icy, you'll have to move your training program into the school gym or run in place at home.

GLOSSARY

ACCELERATION ZONE—In relay races, a portion of the track that is 10 yards in length and one lane in width, and within which the outgoing runner builds up speed.

ANCHOR—The member of a relay team who is last to compete in a race.

ANCHOR LEG—The final leg of a relay race.

BATON—The hollow, tubelike object, about a foot in length, that is passed from one runner to another in a relay race.

BLOCKS—See Starting blocks.

CROSS-COUNTRY—Distance running over hills, unpaved roads, through wooded areas, and other such terrain.

EXCHANGE ZONE—In relay races, a portion of the track that is 20 yards in length and one lane in width, and within which the baton must be passed.

FALSE START—Movement by a competitor across the starting line or off the blocks before the starting signal pistol is fired.

FARTLEK—A method of training in which the runner alternates periods of sprinting with those of running and jogging over cross-country terrain.

FLATS—Lightweight training shoes without any spikes.

HIGH HURDLES—A race over hurdles that are 39 inches in height.

INTERMEDIATE HURDLES—A race over hurdles that are 36 inches in height.

INTERVAL TRAINING—Alternately sprinting and jogging over set distances.

KICK—A runner's final burst of speed at the end of a race.

LAP—One complete circuit of a track; also, to overtake and build one's lead over a competitor by one full circuit of the track.

LEAD LEG—In hurdling, the leg that goes first over the hurdles.

LEG—The portion of a relay race that each member of the relay team must cover.

LOW HURDLES—A race over hurdles that are 30 or 33 inches in height.

MARATHON—A race of 26 miles, 385 yards, that is usually run over public roads closed to traffic.

MEDLEY RELAY—A relay race with legs of unequal lengths.

RELAY—A race between teams, usually with four members to a team, which is run in four stages called legs. Each member of each team runs one leg.

SCRATCH START—A race start in which the runners line up straight across the track.

SPLITS—The recorded times for a runner at specific intervals of a race; for example, every quarter mile in a mile race.

SPRINT—A race run at top speed from start to finish.

STAGGERED START—A race start in which runners are assigned starting points that serve to compensate for the unequal distances to be run. The starting point for each lane from the inside to the outside is progressively farther ahead.

STARTING BLOCKS—Adjustable supports or pedals mounted on either side of a metal shaft which enable a runner to brace her feet for a fast start in a sprint race.

TAPE—The length of string or yarn stretched across the track several feet directly above the finish line that serves to aid the officials in determining the race winner.

TRAILING LEG—In hurdling, the leg that goes last over the hurdles.

TRIAL HEAT—A preliminary contest held to eliminate competitors from the final race, for which there are too many runners to compete at one time.